How To expand Your Small Business:

The Secret To Monetary Freedom

By

Shulamite Happiness

Copy Right © by Shulamite Happiness, 2023. All Right Reserved.

Table of Contents

Introduction

Every business owner aspires to success, yet the majority are unsure of the best course of action. This book opens your eyes to realizing business success.

It takes vision, resiliency, and strategic thinking to succeed in business and entrepreneurship. Understanding the fundamentals of startup advice, marketing tactics, financial management, and career assistance will greatly increase your chances of success whether you're a young entrepreneur or aspiring business professional.

Moreover, your Value matters because your self-perception affects who you become. Self-value refers to how you view and regard yourself; it is dependent on the thoughts and assumptions you have about yourself, which can be challenging to alter. This could also be referred to as self-esteem.

Your sense of self-worth can influence whether you:

• Like and respect yourself as a person.

• Be able to make decisions and assert yourself.

• Recognize your strengths.

• Be willing to try new or challenging things.

• Be kind to yourself

• Be able to move past mistakes without unfairly blaming yourself.

• Be willing to take the time you need for yourself.

• Believe you matter and are deserving of happiness.

Chapter One

Value

The characteristic that makes something appealing or valuable. The significance accorded to anything. It also represents an assessment of something's value.

Value can be perceived from a variety of angles, and it can signify different things to different professions, but it always comes to mean something precious or of high regard.

Something is valued when you believe it to be significant and worthwhile. For instance, if you appreciate someone's viewpoint, you'll consult them for guidance before making a significant choice.

Value refers to how much something is worth, either financially or in terms of significance. It can also mean "determine how much something is worth," as in a prize with a $200 value. As a verb, it denotes "holding something in high regard," as in "I value our friendship."

The Self-Value Rules

1. The Yes rule

In life, we frequently say "no." It's simpler than attempting to pay attention to and comprehend what another person is asking of us. For instance, we frequently reject novel concepts out of a fear of the unknown. The concept of "yes," however, allows us to halt, pay attention, and go ahead from what someone else has to offer.

2. Accepting Mistakes Rules

The feeling of guilt and embarrassment that comes with mistakes may truly overwhelm us, but if we embrace them and accept that everyone makes mistakes, we're less likely to linger on them or let them trip us up. Was this error indeed the end of the world, you could ask? Obviously not.

3. Don't be afraid to be yourself

Being authentic can improve other aspects of your life, just as it can boost your performance. So let go of whatever guilt or concern you may have about not understanding. Show off the elements of yourself that you might be tempted to conceal. And be free to be who you are around your friends, coworkers, classmates, and family. It may be challenging to embrace radical acceptance and self-love, but constantly reminding yourself that your voice matters.

3Hs that ensure achievement

You must effectively use your three (H)s, which are:

1. The Head: Read more to expand your horizons. Be informed; if not, you risk becoming deformed. Attend seminars, workshops, etc.

2. The Hand: Use your hand actively by doing something. Start something, no matter how small, and take action.

3. The Heart: Make wise decisions, make plans, and be positive. Despite the fact that it may not seem possible, have faith in your ability to succeed since the mouth speaks from an abundance of the heart.

How to radically alter your sense of self through personal development.

A reason to change can always be found.

I made the choice to "change & finally improve myself" roughly five years ago.

Despite the fact that everything was so chaotic, it motivated me to take steps that allowed me to begin my life and reinvent myself.

I used to be a restless, depressed, and even anxious young girl who tried to do everything correctly but failed miserably because I had any real drive. I felt overwhelmed by the ongoing issues in my life, which finally led to my apathy and laziness. I simply didn't know how to start or even where to start.

Everything looked to be so challenging, exhausting, and terrifying. Living with constant anxiety and lack of motivation was my daily routine.

Does that sound like the situation you're in right now? If that's the case, I want to assure you that it's changeable!.

So when I realized that I didn't want to live a terrible existence, everything changed for me. I made the decision to stop playing the victim.

I began reading about personal development, cleaning up my bad attitude, reshaping my nervous thoughts, making plans for changes, and finally acting.

Small adjustments and approaches helped me overcome my anxiety and develop braver thinking, bigger ambitions, wider smiles, and a more positive outlook on life once I began working on myself.

I rapidly developed a passion for personal development since it inspired me to believe that things could improve.

Make a mental shift, learn to evolve, and start experiencing lovely things in your life.

Chapter Two

How to Add Value to Your Life

Adhere to your Passion

Ensure that you are doing what you enjoy. And while this might bring about significant upheaval in your life, try to accept it and go on. Keep in mind that change can magnify your journey. It's okay if your passion doesn't always align with your employment and professional life. Just as long as you make an effort to focus as much of your energy as you can on the things you value. Enjoy the pleasure that comes from the things you are passionate about.

Know yourself

Examine how your behavior influence others, you will realize how potency you are. And it's crucial to communicate what you want in return to the outside world. Therefore, be careful while making decisions that can affect other people because if you send out bad energy, it will eventually find its way back to you. But seriously, how can you expect others to treat you well if you treat them poorly yourself? A newfound capacity to appreciate things for who they are comes with self-awareness. Like, look around and try to be grateful that you're actually at a bright position. This is taking into account the periods when things aren't as awful and acting appropriately to improve those circumstances.

Set daily objectives

Every morning, make attainable goals for the day. If you set realistic daily goals for yourself, you'll be able to celebrate your accomplishments each day. Your outlook can be much improved by incorporating this constructive challenge and reward system into your daily routine. If you can find happiness each day, you are succeeding in life. Setting impossible standards for yourself will only make you feel depressed when you fall short. Make modest goals, then successfully accomplish them.

Tolerance for change

It could be making a professional move or removing yourself from a harmful relationship. Whatever the change, accepting it and embracing it can greatly reduce the stress in your life. Accept that you must go along with life and make an effort to have fun while doing so. Live your best life and be more adaptable to change.

Chapter Three

Wealth: What Is It?

Wealth is the worth of all the valuable properties' someone, associate or a community possess.

A nation or people are said to be rich and prosperity when there's accumulation of wealth. Wealth is an asset, it appreciates and yield more value if properly handled.

Everyone perspectives on wealth are different, some view wealth as real estate investment, for others it is profit yielded from an investment.

Even while it could appear difficult to accumulate wealth, but with determination and consistency it can be achieved.

Remember that creating wealth is a process that takes time.

How To Increase Wealth

Check out the three suggestions listed below for ways to increase your wealth.

1. Boost Your Earnings

Having several sources of income is the most essential step to accumulating wealth, whether you're just starting out or going through a shift. Here are a few strategies for quickly boosting your income and accumulating wealth.

2. Start a Business

The richest people in the world are business founders rather than employees. Two requirements for wealth creation are met by entrepreneurship: income and strong returns on accumulated wealth. Start your business if it has the potential to boost your income.

It doesn't have to be an enormous business. You can manage to launch a small business and provide the services you are expertise at. For instance, you can possibly start an online-based business by reason of the development of the internet. You can hire somebody to run the business if you're too busy to do it yourself.

3. Accept well-paid employment

To support yourself and to pay your costs, you can apply for a high-paying work. The average salary for more than 100 occupations is at least $80,000 annually. Medical professionals, managers, nurses, and engineers are a few examples of highly compensated professionals.

Some of these careers, meanwhile, are exceedingly pricey. The required education could take a long time to finish, and it might take even longer before you start making a good living. Before choosing a profession, you should take into account all of these criteria. Make sure that whichever professional choice you choose won't leave you with excessive debt.

Run side businesses

You don't have to rely solely on your salary even if you have a job. To boost your revenue, you can successfully operate a side business. You can engage in this during your free period.

As long as you have internet access, you may run a number of successful side businesses online. These include:

- becoming a virtual assistant, writing and editing for a living.
- Copywriting.
- Coaching and consulting clients online. Web design, app development, coding, etc.

Other side jobs without internet connection include:

- Working as a shopper.
- Working as a part-time driver for a ride-sharing or delivery service.
- Working as a part-time instructor at a nearby college.
- Working as a part-time gym instructor.
- Working as a freelance bookkeeper, tax preparer, or tutor.

4. Develop Your Skills

You can increase your income and investment returns in two different ways. Either you may earn more money or reduce your spending. Most individuals overlook the second as they concentrate on the first. By developing your skill set, you can raise your income. This can entail earning a diploma, an MBA, or a specialized title, which can all lead to a promotion and a raise in pay.

5. Spend Less

Another idea to accumulation of wealth is by saving. It's appropriate to start saving once you have enough money to cover your essential expenses. Keep in mind that frequent tiny savings add up to big wealth over time.

6. Establish a Budget

Your financial plan should include projections of your expenses and revenue. A budget is an important tool for developing wealth. It provides you with an overview of your spending, highlighting areas where you might make savings.

It is suggested to make a fresh budget each month in order to keep a workable one. A person that doesn't budget is income by spending money carelessly will probably have a severe financial collapse in the future.

7. Create a reserve fund.

Emergency fund kits help you be ready for unforeseen circumstances like losing your job. Without emergency cash, such events can throw off your wealth-building efforts. Selling the investment or accruing debt are two typical consequences.

Debt causes your money to start eroding. You'll also be required to pay interest on the debt. The capital and interest you would have otherwise earned are lost if you sell your investment. Create an emergency fund as a backup to cover unforeseen expenses to avoid such situations.

8. Live below your Financial Resources

Spending too much money might seriously hinder your capacity to accumulate wealth. Spend less on irrational expenses like eating out, purchasing luxury clothing, and taking frequent vacations. Although being thrifty can be monotonous and unfulfilling, you'll eventually accumulate money and find it to be enjoyable.

9. Invest After you've established a monthly savings target, you should start investing. You receive more money in return when you invest your money. You can amass enormous wealth over time by investing your salary in the stock market, real estate, and retirement plans etc.

Chapter 4

Marketing Techniques

Effective marketing techniques are essential for luring and keeping clients in the cutthroat environment of today. Determine your target audience first, then learn about their wants and preferences. Create a memorable brand narrative that connects with your audience and sets you apart from the competition. Use a multichannel marketing strategy to increase your audience by utilizing influencer partnerships, social media, digital platforms, and content marketing. To improve marketing campaigns and spur growth, continuously examine data and modify your methods.

It's possible to explore entrepreneurship within already-established organizations, so it's not just confined to founding your own business. It is essential for ambitious business professionals to have a broad skill set and accumulate real-world experience. Look for opportunities to work in a variety of positions, develop a strong professional network, and make an investment in ongoing education. Accept challenges and take on tasks that require you to use your skills in new ways, so you can learn new things. Consult mentors and business authorities who can offer insightful advice and aid in directing your career.

Strategies to work on:

Setting up a business necessitates critical thinking, tenacious organization, and meticulous record-keeping.

• It's critical to be aware of your rivals' strategies and adopt or enhance their winning ones.

• When you start your own business, you'll almost probably find that you have to work harder than you would for someone else. Be prepared to give up certain things in your personal life.

• Providing your consumers with excellent service is essential to winning their loyalty and keeping their business.

Chapter 5

How to conduct your small business professionally

The entire planet is vast and chaotic. A sea of mega businesses can easily drown out tiny businesses, leaving them unable to leave a lasting imprint. In a cutthroat industry, many firms want assistance in projecting a professional image.

Three Ideas You Must Know to Look Professional

Fundamentally, professionalism is about being able to meet the needs of your clients. In order to achieve product-market fit, you must create a good or service that is required by a certain target market. But simply being good at your work is insufficient. You must project an image of competence in your work.

Here are three business concepts you need to know in order to present a professional image.

1. Marketing fundamentals. Business expansion is a result of marketing. You must let people know about your goods or services. Make it known and publish material for it. Start promoting your stuff.

Small-scale social media posts, blog articles, and YouTube video essays are all examples of content marketing. You can pursue many different types of content marketing, but it's actually best to just pick one that you find appealing.

The simple fact that people instinctively start to trust those who openly share their skills on the internet is the main reason content marketing will help you appear more professional. Just consider it! You are likely to have at least some faith in the subject-matter expert when you find a web page on Google after conducting a search for a term.

2. Fundamentals of branding. People frequently refer to well-managed brands when describing enterprises that have a professional appearance. Branding is the process of continuously communicating the same message to your target market.

3. The fundamentals of customer service. The user experience can be defined as how customers feel while interacting with your company. Thinking about the customer's journey when they interact with your organization can help you to grasp this the simplest way possible.

Techniques For Making Your Expanding Small Business Appear Even Bigger

1. Create a strong logo.

All major businesses have websites, and you ought to have one as well. A logo can help your brand become instantly identifiable because people tend to notice images before words.

2. Don't skimp on your audio, video, or photography.

Investing in quality photography, videography, and audio equipment is one of the simplest ways to give your company a more professional appearance. Most of these things are also not very pricey. A modest investment in good lighting can significantly raise the caliber of your pictures and movies.

3. Establish and regularly update your social media accounts.

54 percent of social media users check up businesses on the platform. You may increase your visibility to those who use social media to conduct brand research by simply having a presence there—not an extensive following, just a presence.

4. Employ Reliable Branding

Your branding should convey a unified look and message across all platforms. Consistency in branding not only strengthens your image but also gives you an air of professionalism and business sense. Make sure the colors, graphics, and logos on your stationery, website, social media sites, and storefront match.

Even your packaging and stationery should be consistent with your brand. While not every logo and picture you have must be used on every platform, everything should be consistent. If it doesn't, you could come out as irresponsible or untidy.

5. Possess an exclusive business phone number

60 percent of customers still choose to call businesses instead of contacting them online, proving that phone calls are still relevant in the digital age. Given the frequency of phone calls, you should make sure your business has a dedicated number.

If you use your personal phone for business, you can treat callers too carelessly. To use a new number on the same devices, you can either choose a landline for your business or use a Voice over Internet Protocol (VoIP) service.

6. Obtain a Business Email Account.

Using a Yahoo or Gmail account for business purposes can come off as unprofessional. It appears that you are using a personal address, and since anyone could own that account, it may appear insecure. On the other hand, using an email address that is the same as your domain immediately gives you a more businesslike appearance.

7. Be Careful Not to Relax About Payment

It can be tempting to overlook some clients' late or missed payments when you're just starting out. Although it makes sense to want to come across as approachable or informal, professionalism also includes getting paid on time. Create a system for swiftly and professionally billing consumers.

8. Dress to Succeed

Your staff' appearance affects how clients and potential business partners see you. It's possible that people won't take you seriously as a business if your dress code is too casual. Even if a suit or full uniform may not be required every day, your appearance should nonetheless be professional.

It might be sufficient to just require business casual clothes for staff. Customers can more easily recognize personnel if they are wearing name tags or plain shirts with branding. There is no one-size-fits-all approach here, so make sure you look professional and wear attire appropriate for your line of work.

9. Establish a Stronger First Impression

A first impression can convey a lot of information. However, you should want to come across as a professional business above all else. It will make you appear more credible and serious in the eyes of clients and other businesses.

10. Make use of a P.O.

You should not simply pay attention to your email address. You need a place for partners and suppliers to send stuff, even when customers might not contact you via mail. You can utilize a P.O. box for your mail if you don't have a physical storefront or office space.

Conclusion

The fields of business and entrepreneurship are dynamic and constantly changing, need ongoing adaptation and education. You are giving yourself the skills you need to succeed in business by adopting startup advise, putting good marketing ideas into practice, maintaining good financial management, and looking for career counseling. Keep in mind that ideas alone won't guarantee success; you also need to execute them with commitment, tenacity, and strategic thinking. Take advantage of chances, embrace the entrepreneurial spirit, and pave your way to a wealthy future.

www.ingramcontent.com/pod-product-compliance
Lightning Source LLC
Chambersburg PA
CBHW060909260726
48661CB00008B/3555